Millville, Through Our Eyes

Millville, Through Our Eyes
Copyright © 2025
Cover Art by Kevin Jordan 2025

All rights reserved. Blue Jade Press, LLC retains the right to reprint this book. Permission to reprint poems from this collection must be obtained by the author.

ISBN- 978-1-961043-11-4

Published by:

Blue Jade Press, LLC

Blue Jade Press, LLC
Vineland, NJ 08360
www.bluejadepress.com

To all the Poets, Artists, and Musicians of High Street,
Thank you for making the magic

Rebecca Bonham

The Arts are alive in Millville! This collaboration between Blue Jade Press and An Octopus's Garden proves it!

As the owner of An Octopus's Garden for the last 15 years, I have represented over 150 artists, painters, sculptors, jewelry makers, poets, and musicians.

This anthology includes fifteen poets, past and present, who have performed, supported, and enriched the Arts community with their work and their voices.

Come fall in love with Millville again....
through our eyes!

                                            Maryann Kuntz

Table of Contents

Unlikely, Zeus Cruz	1
Cattails, Zeus Cruz	3
Ocean Symphony, Richard Zielinski	5
Last of the Jersey Cowboys, Richard Zielinski	6
Yes, Richard Zielinski	7
Now and Forever, Trinity O'Brien	8
She is Me, Trinity O'Brien	9
Gem, Trinity O'Brien	10
A Conversatio,n Rebecca Bonham & John Bongo	11
Deaf, Kate Hart Nardone	13
Clouds on a Trampoline, Kate Hart Nardone	14
Exactly Enough, Kate Hart Nardone	15
Fate's House, Rory Danielle Wilson	17
Punching Bag, Maddie Friel	18
Landmine, Maddie Friel	19
My Mask, Michael Cohen	21
The Grind, Michael Cohen	23
Local Color, Mark Soifer	25
The Lights of the Prison, Mark Soifer	26
City of Wires, Mark Soifer	28
Stone Warriors, Robert Griffiths	30
Lady Justice, Robert Griffiths	31
Sole to Soul, Kevin Jordan	32
Better Man, Kevin Jordan	33
This Song, Kevin Jordan	34
Open Mic in Millville, Mark Schardine	35
Cedar Plank Steak, Mark Schardine	36
An Old Coffee Drinker Ponders, Mark Schardine	37
On First Viewing "Starry Night", Renee Rasinger	38
Gravity, Renee Rasinger	39
To the Bitch, Renee Rasinger	40
At the Mall, Alma Cole Pesiri	41
Feel the Beat, Alma Cole Pesiri	42
Millville Newcomers Club, Alma Cole Pesiri	43

Unlikely
Zeus Cruz

Look and behold
From the depths of the Holly City
A poet from 9th Street
Who bares no resemblance to a muse
So they say

From his darken features
And his mortality riddled
With imperfections, worn and chiseled
To his somber, solemn expressions
Provides the reflection
Of an outlook that seems abysmal

Yet he designs his dreams
To the constellations
Built within the multitude of stars
He writes sonnets from experience
That are woven into patches
That encompasses his many scars

His verses are forged
From flames so potent
That it gives even hell its warmth
He showcases to all
A different kind of poet's art
Beneath the grime
A dreamer's soul
A mind that weaves its magical spell

His words, though rough, make spirits whole
A hidden depth, a secret well
As he travels through a labyrinth

From the outskirts of High Street
To the underpass
That leads to the Sharp Street Park
So he can be one with his thoughts
And somehow mold his concepts into ingenuity

The lesson written here
Echoes to the notion
Not to rush to judgement
And be fooled by sight

For poets come in every guise
For he writes his poems with all of his might
A testament to hidden skies
That barricade the brilliance of the sun
For out of the darkness
He pushes through glimpses of light

For likely
This poet is just like you

Cattails
Zeus Cruz

My spirit aches with torment
As I journey through this bog of deceit
As my footprints lead to the unknown
A trail made I wish no one to follow

Feel as if I am now baptized
As I'm splashed with the water of truth
I used to cleanse myself of the mud stains
That signifies my past mistakes

The swamp of memories
Now resembles a confession booth
As the dirt of my transgressions
Offset my reflection
For I do not recognize myself anymore

I find comfort hiding behind the cattails
So no one can acknowledge my presence
For I am ashamed of what I have become
I only show glimpses of myself
In between the spaces

As the cattails sway from the harsh breeze
And yet delight and bewilderment
Becomes etched across my face
As I discover a trace of steps
Just to the side of me
And I realize
I am not alone
In this trek of redemption

The air was foul
And now has a pleasant aroma of hope
Once numb to my senses
I now feel the warmth of vindication

The sunlight is piercing through
The droplets laying upon the cattails
Creating miniature prisms of life
Back into my soul

And as I walk out from behind
What I deemed as a barricade
Amazement came within my view
And brought tears to my eyes
As I saw my loved ones run towards me
To embrace me
And this is the moment I knew

There is such a thing
As a second chance

Ocean Symphony
Richard Zielinski

The noise!
Unseen waves of water and sand
Boom over the dune
How the soft water thunders!
How the foam whispers in retreat
It's the world's song
Gaia's breath
Crossing a vast ocean
Echoing off the backs
Of sperm whales
Borne by Bluefin tuna
Conditioned by jellyfish rhythms
Played off the sides of silvered sardines
Inspired by a doting moon

Last of the Jersey Cowboys
Richard Zielinski

I am an old cowhand
who's never seen the Rio Grande
my hoss was the sofa's arm
imaginary reins in my hand
we'd ride the Jersey trails
pine pollen blown by gusts
like a 20 mule team train
kicking up Death Valley dust
I rode with the Cisco Kid
me and Pancho side by side
I carried Gene's guitar
in case a song came up on the ride
and though Hoppy wore that big black hat
he was on the side of the good
and when Rowdy raced to head off the herd
why, you just knew that he would
so bury me out in the Jersey pitch pines
in my slick Roy Rogers shirt
Gene Autry guitar by my side
in that sandy pinelands dirt
for cowboy is a state of mind
it lives inside of you
thanks to all the tv stars
that you never outgrew

Yes
Richard Zielinski, for DL

Yes there's one more kiss, don't worry
though the lips grow cold and the will grows weary
love is a fire, love is an ember
though eyes grow dim, the belly remembers
and yes (oh yes) I remember
the twisty ways, the turns, meanders
the crooked paths love loves to wander
we stumble happily ever after
as the mirror wryly laughs its laughter
and yes (oh yes) I still remember

Now and Forever
Trinity O'Brien

Gentle hands and a warm heart
I'm caught in the net of your love
Safe in your arms
Comfortable in this state of vulnerability

I believe love is a choice
A choice you made easy
Growing together as one
Flourishing into the garden of life

Your eyes
Deep and rich
I gaze into them and see our future ahead
Dinner on the table
Children running into the embrace of a loving father

I love you now
I can't wait for forever

She is Me
Trinity O'Brien

Graceful walk
Effortless movement
She leaps past the obstacles of life
Distracting herself with each flowing stride

Releasing herself through every stretch
Every breath-taking emotion-shaking routine
She has found creative freedom
She has gained self-expression

She is me

An audience awaits
Ready to watch and feel
They can see directly through me
Like a window to my beating heart

Gem
Trinity O'Brien

The ray of sunshine that walked into my life
The breath of fresh air
Giving strength
Encouraging growth
Helping me stand firm

Lifting me up
Through the good, bad, and ugly times
She has seen it all

No judgement
No betrayal
Always guiding
Always faithful

She deserves everything beautiful and good
More than this world could ever offer

She is a radiant gem
That shines brighter than them all

A Conversation in Poetry
Rebecca Bonham & John E. Bongo

5db Window

It was that absence of noise,
I never knew it was there.
The cricket becomes clearer but not louder.
That sound screams at some,
through their digitally processed ears.
For me, it's dull and faded,
faintly echoing the laughter of the past.
I fail to grasp those echoes
Happiness slips from my fingers, leaving a mess of me.
           (Rebecca Bonham)

John's Reply

The cavern framed in Wine-Vines, Vines that wear the
"other" cover of dusk like a Michael Jackson's glove.
The light, it dawns enough shiny, refraction, distraction
to at least get you nearby. But, how good are you at
Dreaming? The Labyrinth beneath—never been, but I
hear good things while; I use the ceiling of heaven as
monkey bars during my inversion table meditation.
The comfort zone—it's tai-ji, going across the ball park,
Where the officer exercises his K-9 best friend. I've left
them to their moment since, The contour of the inferior,
it has character, A character, A steam, Esteem You guide
them to their window, their secret place, A reflection of
the sun in your lake, which they enjoy in its still, Still, a
century of will could erode here while you drink Diet
Pepsi in the shade And, friend zone Xanax.
        (John E. Bongo, April 12, 2013)

John Bongo passed suddenly November 24, 2013

Silence
There is a disruption in the force
My five-decibel window closed,
While I was drinking Pepsi by the lake.
We will meet in the matrix, my friend.
To have our sunset dual.
I shall be victorious, or let you win.

(Rebecca Bonham)

City Tears
I wept for the chaos, churning me, burning me, leaving me standing on the sidewalk looking at the multicolored chalk lines of your soul. They float spinning me, dipping me, sweeping my hair across the rain washed gutters. Dripping, I stand to wipe the sandy gray drops from my chest, where they cling to my shirt, reminding me of you.

(Rebecca Bonham)

Deaf
Kate Hart Nardone

Sounds of voices
audible and detailed
anticipating a response

I, the recipient
deafened by the ringing of my own mind's rhetoric
exhausted by the images and rewinds of my soul's
wounds, worries, and wonders

Uncomfortable
awkward
ignorant

I saw your mouth moving
I'm sorry, can you repeat that one more time?

Clouds on a Trampoline
Kate Hart Nardone

What I wouldn't give to be there again!
Laying on the black mat circle with a metal frame

Just three girls watching clouds on a trampoline

A unicorn
A flamingo
A pirate ship

Each taking turns explaining what we see
Comically arguing our perspectives
Watching the forms morph and change
With each tick of the clock

"Now it's a robot!"
"No, it looks like Dad!"
"Oh, stop, it's definitely a zombie!"

Our laughter lightly bouncing us in rhythm
Stolen earthly moments of perfection
The kind of moments that make life bearable
That make life beautiful

Us three girls, watching clouds on a trampoline

Exactly Enough
Kate Hart Nardone

I am an imperfectly wonderful human
A magical female
An indigenous warrior
A vicious lioness

I am the student of my parents
The witness to my husband's life
The nurturer of my offspring
A servant to my species

I am all and none of those things

I am a perfectly flawed being
A broken child
An emotional wrecking ball
An insecure coward

I am the rebellious prodigal
The villain in someone's life story
The invisible provider
An embarrassment to my comrades

I am all and none of those things

How then, can one describe me?

I am a temporary body
Fragile bones and ink covered skin

I am an empathetic soul
Heartfelt laughter and unstoppable tears
I am God's detailed spiritual creation
Suffering the temporary to help crowd eternity

My three defined selves
all available for use or misuse
And…I have…used and misused them all

But am not defined by my actions,
Vocalizations,
Subscriptions,
Beliefs,
Or contradictions
I am a jigsaw puzzle with missing pieces
A faith and doubt filled disciple of Christ
I am both sorry and without regret

I am the eyes of my father
And the strength of my mother

I am an artist of beautiful chaos
The scribe of transparent victories and vulnerable tragedies
The helping hands of maternal journeys
The voice and healer of the insignificant creatures of this world

I am immeasurable
Always without limit
And often, without excuse

I need to be less and I need to be more

And yet, I am exactly enough

Fate's House
Rory Danielle Wilson

Spinning is my head
atop the springs and sheets of gold
my love has dived between the moons
in painted words that climb the sky
to reach bright stars
with eyes covered tight
blindly dancing to fingers pretty
and trapping daydreams with words of tomorrow
riding on joyful tears
that possess the sweat smell of love
crawling down my face on flights of stairs
tumbling across the pale desert
who knows the touch of angels palms
and the sound of souls being freed
so, underneath my feet
radiant voices has whispered
and told me of fairytale houses built by our minds
to protect our fragile bodies and make a place
to live the story that was written by fate
so long ago….

Punching Bag
Maddie Friel

Your soft, but hard
Easy to punch
Hit.hit.hit.
Your purpose is to take other people's hits
Hit.hit.hit.
Everyone takes a turn, and nobody hits just once
Hit.hit.hit.
You take it with a smile, never questioning
Always forgiving the hits; in time for the next one
Hit.hit.hit.
You expect the hits
You don't think bad about the people who hit
This is your purpose
To be hit
Why would someone not hit you?
Hit.hit.hit.
Do they think you cant handle it,
Cause you can
Hit.hit.hit.
Your forced to think…
If no one is hitting you now,
And your alive, and surviving
Hit.hit.hit
Did you ever need to be hit in the first place?
Hit.hit.hit.
Then you think…
……………………….
Do I still take the hits?
……………….
Hit… Hit…. Hit…

Landmine
Maddie Friel

The bomb goes off, once, you think,
Fuck…. That sucked, but at least it is over
Then you step again, and it goes off again,
Fuck…. That sucked
I won't step there no more,
You take another step,
Boom!! bomb goes off
Fuck….
You take another step,
Boom!! bomb goes off
Fuck….
That's when you realize,
he turned your brain into a land mind,
And you have no idea where the next bomb is,
Fuck…
You try to go slow, and think about every move,
Then you hear something,
It triggers the bomb, and
Boom! …. It goes off
Fuck…
You try to reason with the contrapment
Telling it this is illogical, and impossible
Nothing works
Once its triggered
Boom!!
Fuck…
You try again
Boom!!
You try again, but differently
Boom!!

You start to jump on the mines you know,
because at least you know what that bomb does, and looks like,
Fuck…
Each Boom takes more of you
Fuck…
You step…
and step…
and step…
trying to get to the other side,
Boom!!
Boom!!
Boom!!
Fuck…..
You stop stepping,
You stand still,
You don't care about getting to the other side,
You just don't want to set off another bomb,

But then you hear something,
And you're triggered,
fuck…….

My Mask
Michael Cohen, ©2024 CohenWorks

From this day on, I wear a mask
the image of my face
it's the only one of its kind
in the entire human race!

It smiles when I'm not able
relaying fairy tales and fables
it's present at the Christmas table
welcoming Bill, and Phil and Mabel

It offers pleasantries at meals
and poker facing deals
hiding all that's real
promoting false ideals

It's
pliable
reliable
it's lies are undeniable
it's deception unperceptable
hiding feeling reprehensible
it's quite contrite in principle
my mask makes me invincible

From this day on I wear a mask
a disguise of my design
a mirror of my visage
it leaves all truth behind

Don't ask me how I'm doing
I'll always answer "Great!"
even on the road to ruin
my mask won't hesitate

Although I guffaw with glee
it really isn't me
I only wish my mask was all that I can be

It's
Malleable
Infallible
Indestructible
Tax Deductible
it's grateful on the days, the days that I get paid
and it feigns ecstasy when I'm getting laid

It lays beside me when I sleep
and in the morning I fill it deep

It is my one true friend
in who I can depend
I'll wear my trusted mask until the bitter end
I learned my lesson well
keep secrets close to my chest
and to guard a hurting heart
a mask is always best

The Grind
Michael Cohen, ©2010 CohenWorks

In the morning when I wake up
and I think of what's ahead I convince myself
that it's ok to spend another five in bed

I think of all the years that passed
and the life that I have led
I think of all I could have been
and what I should have done instead

Morning is a strange time
there are fewer minutes in an hour
I realize I'm way behind
and I still need to shave and shower

On the highway cars are standing still
like cows left out to graze
while the city streets are being filled
like rats caught in a maze,
and I know I've had my fill
it's too much for my mind,
but I am stuck and out of luck
I'm no match for the Grind.

The broken mirror stares at me with a sullen icy glare
my eyes are gazing back at me as if I weren't there

My spirit stumbles in the wind
through the forest of the blind
although I try I just can't win
I'm no match for the Grind

I 9 to 5 it every day
and my weekends are a bore

A week per year I get away
but I come back for more

The calendar throw insults
and the clock he joins right in
they mock my sad existence
and inability to win,
the more I fight
the more my hair turns white
it's too much for my mind
I'll shut the light
and get some sleep tonight
but tomorrow it's back to the Grind

Local Color
Mark Soifer

The weed flowers-
The ones whose names are seldom
Mentioned— if they have names-
Lean high above the grass
On skinny extensions…
Spread here by wind
And subtle vibrations of earth
They nod above litter
Rippled by passing cars…
And when they eventually die
There is no trace of death-
Just a place for rain to spread-
A place for snow to settle…

The Lights of the Prison
Mark Soifer

Driving this old South Jersey road
At night is a cheerless occupation-
What with the miles of darkened woods,
Abandoned homes, blank windows and
Mute, indifferent telephone poles-
Until finally my car takes the bend
And passes the State Correctional
Facility at Leesburg with its long
Rows of orange and yellow lights going
Nowhere—And I think to myself; what's
This prison for if not to cheer my soul-
Imprisoned in this car, imprisoned in
A body with a mind that's going nowhere…

The City of Wires

Photo provided by the family of Mark Soifer

City of Wires
Mark Soifer

A few
miles
past
the blinker
on
Route 55
there
is
a place
where reams
of
high tension
wires
meet

A way
station
for
brief
conferences
following
long, slack
stretches
over woods
& winter fields

wired
fences
keep out
unwired
strangers

There
is a steady hum
of impulses

Vacant
clouds
watch

Stone Warriors
Robert Griffiths

On the corner where the cold wind blows
he stands, forgotten, in tattered clothes
his eyes hold battles no one sees
lost in his memories, down on his knees

He served with pride in days long past
where brotherhood held, and time moved fast
now the streets are his only friend
a fight for warmth that has no end

Loneliness echoes in his chest
where once he stood among the best
now shadows are the company kept
in doorways where the city slept

A flag once waved above his head
now cardboard serves as his bed
the medals rust, the glory gone
but the pain of war keeps marching on

He dreams of home, but what is that?
not in the alley, nor in his hat
it's lost somewhere with his comrades' cheer
drowned by silence, soaked in tears

So he wanders, heart full of scars
beneath the endless, uncaring stars
a hero once, now just a face
homeless, forgotten–a veteran displaced

Lady Justice the Mother of America
Robert Griffiths

Lady Justice, poised with grace
in your steadfast stance, I find my place
with scales in hand so finely balanced
you embody truth pure and valiant

Your blindfold shields you from deceit
unmoved by power, fame or feat
impartial gaze no favor shown
you stand for all, yet stand alone

In the sword, you hold I see my might–
to cleave through wrong and make things right
your edge is share your aim is true
and in your strength, my heart renews

It's not the force but what you fight
a world where all can claim their right
I love you for the path you pave
for justice pure and lives you save

Lady Justice firm and fair
in your judgement none despair
through you I see the world's rebirth
a love that's bound to all of worth

Sole to Soul
Kevin Jordan

His soul is tattered
beat up and torn
like the soles of his shoes
all shattered and worn
undesired by many
sought out by few
his soul has holes
like the ones in his shoes
been walked on
beyond repair
been walked on
does anyone really care?

Better
Kevin Jordan

I wish I knew how to be
a better person
a better man
a better dad

I wish I took the time
and paid attention
If I only would have

I wish I knew how to be
a better man
better friend
better brother
better pop-pop

There is still time
Maybe I will

This Song
Kevin Jordan

This song takes me back
to a simpler time
a long time ago
T-shirts and faded cut offs
and you at the swimming hole
the pond and a fishing pole
a 69 Chevy pick up
down a long dirt road
a transistor radio playing
in the kitchen and you
this song reminds me
of yesterday
and you

Open Mic in Millville
Mark Schardine

Make sure to sign up
You do have poems ready
We want to hear you
First, let others speak
Allow their thoughts to wander
The pleasures of life
Love, rivalries, jealousies,
Joy, sorrow, laughter, and tears
Find inspiration
Let others' words challenge you
Push your thoughts forward
Jumble them organize them
Add music to your own words
When time comes to speak
Give each word its full value
Express each nuance
Speak while also implying
Then watch as your friends ponder
When you fall silent
Your words will drift in the air
No one will forget

Cedar Plank Steak
Mark Schardine

Thick spice-covered steak
Interspersed with bits of fat
Lies on a soaked plank
Charcoal briquettes burn
Make the grill too hot to touch
Give off heat, smoke, steam
The plank on the grill
Gives off steam, slowly dries out
Gently cooks your steak
As you sit and chat
Curry melts and coats the meat
Its scent drifts past you
When your plate arrives
Slice into tender moist steak
Hot, seasoned, garnished.
Leisurely savor
Red meat with a curry kick
This summertime treat

An Old Coffee Drinker Ponders and Plagiarizes T.S. Eliot
Mark Schardine

Oh, I have enjoyed them all already, enjoyed them all
Have consumed in evenings, mornings, afternoons,
I have measured out my life with coffee spoons.
I know the voices issuing a cappuccino call
Beneath the music within a Starbucks room
So how should I presume?

On First Viewing "Starry Night"
Renee Rasinger

Death, one day, may plug
my nose and ears.
Close my eyes with night.
But right now, this dark,
star-breather sky
lashes the land
with its color-tail
in a frieze of fire.
Its blue claws cradle
persimmon bursts that
swirl around my tongue,
crash over my palette,
sucking me down
into a whirlpool
of unnamed stars.
Sealing its mouth
over mine, it breathes
for me, in and out,
out and in, until,
I gasp and spit out
death forever.

Gravity
Renee Rasinger

All that I have ever seen of sky:
this blue silk dress.
these fallen autumn wings.
(Such a rustling—
like wings.)

To the Bitch Who Lived Here Before Me
Renee Rasinger

The layers of grease that coat
the stove and counter do not offend.
Nor does the weird, political junk mail
that arrives daily in your name:
Harpy, Boot-licker, Wheyface.
No, your offense would be
the crows living in the nearby
woods that dive-bomb me
every single time I leave
the house or exit my car.
The food and shiny trinkets
I've left them have no effect at all.
What in the world did you do to them?
Did you run madly across the yard,
swirling your witch broom
to shoo them away?
Or, did you pick up your rifle
and, onion-eyed, blast
black plumage to the sky?
This generational crow-grudge
you gifted me with is murder.
The next-door neighbor said
she can't understand it as
I look nothing like you.

And, having met you once
at the house closing,
I can only say,
"Thank God for that!"

At the Mall
Alma Cole Pesiri

Three happy smiles tossed
Pennies into the fountain

I cried to have lost
That magic to age

Then I thought, why not?

And wished
On a penny

Feel the Beat
Alma Cole Pesiri

Feel the beat
I mean REALLY feel the beat
of the music behind the poetry
weaving between the words
that sing our feelings
while the music
fills the air
that carries the message
we want to hand to you
want to sing to you
want to share with you

interacting while it measures
every nuance that you gather
from the music of our writing
sharing poems, sharing poems

(For Rita Lynn Lyman to read to music)

Millville Newcomers Club
Alma Cole Pesiri

Friends when I was a stranger
giving information,
trust and fun.
a smiling map of the City
with eyes
and
ears
to guide me on my first
hesitant steps
up High Street
and
down
Main

About the Poets

Zeus Cruz is a writer and poet who has published ten books that encompasses the styles of poetry and short stories written in the genres of fantasy, horror, mythology, and sci-fi. Zeus Cruz is the Founder and Creative Director of Olympian Multimedia- a media and production development business and one-half of the production duo AlphaOmega. Along with managing his online store, Zeus also produces for live service audio sensations. AlphaOmega has produced seven albums through the Olympian Multimedia banner and they are available on online music platforms.

Richard Zielinski is a sometime poet, fitful folksy singer-songwriter, avid birder, tai chi/chi gong student and retired jack-of-various-trades. He can often be found birding around South Jersey where he lives. He is the author of the illustrated poem, *The Mean Old Man Who Didn't Like Children* and the poetry collection *Scything*. See more at https://meanoldman.org/

Trinity O'Brien is currently a high school senior about to graduate in May. Trinity is involved in several school activities and is very active in her home church, including volunteering for children's ministries.

She will be attending Rowan College of South Jersey in the fall to begin her journey into Early Childhood Education. Her goal is to be a pre-school teacher. She also planes to be a dance instructor. She wants to do missions work in Asia and assist anti-sex trafficking organizations in rescue and recovery

Rebecca Bonham is a lifelong resident of Southern New Jersey. Her first job (at 9 yrs. old) was working for her Grandparents bookstore, where she would order and display the children's and adolescent sections. She continues her love of art and literature as co-owner of Blue Jade Press, LLC; publishing local authors of all genres.

Rebecca is an active member of the Millville, New Jersey Art's District. She hosts poetry workshops, local author features, and open mics. She has hosted the open mic portion of the Teen Arts Festival in Millville NJ, 2018-2024. She also performs at various open mics in New Jersey. She was published in local literary magazines *L'Spirit* Cumberland Co. College, 2007; "*Disorder III*" and "*Moving beyond Mars*" Red Dashboard, 2017. Her own collection, *Model Poet*" was published in 2021, Blue Jade Press.

John E. Bongo was a poet, musician, artist, creative, friend, supporter of the arts, activist, and an energy too big for this world. He is sadly missed.

Kate Hart Nardone is a five-time published author with many new works in progress. After graduating from Fairton Christian Center Academy, she majored in literature and art at Cumberland County College. She went on to study art history and literature at Harvard University, where she received a certification for mastery in the works of Walt Whitman in 2014. She is a resident studio artist at The Riverfront Renaissance Center for the Arts in Millville, N.J. She is also a certified Birth Doula.

Kate enjoys spending time with her loving husband, Matt, and her four gifted and unique children: Matthew, Christian, Trinity, and Kairi. She stands by the fact that her children are her greatest achievement in life.

Kate currently serves in youth and prayer ministries at her home church. She is also the host of The Hart to Heart Radio Show on AcsendFM.com, Mon-Fri 10am-12pm. She is a proud follower of her Lord and Savior, Jesus Christ.

Rory Danielle Wilson passed away unexpectedly on Oct 12th, 2011 at the young age of only 28 years old. Originally, of Vineland, she was a certified herbalist and massage therapist. Her personal and professional lives were in full flower, and she left behind her a great number of bewildered and grieving family and friends.

Everywhere Rory went, she quickly became known for her joy for living and her sincere interest in the lives of others. Her enthusiasm and energy were infectious and endearing, and she made people glad to be close to her.

Rory Danielle Wilson lived daily life as if it was a special occasion. Her generosity of spirit made her a welcome presence wherever she went and she touched many lives in her brief years. Her motto was "Plant seeds and sing songs." If there is any purpose in the untimely passing of such a spirit, it must be to make us all more grateful for our own precious time on earth.

A full book of Rory's original poetry will be published in 2025.

Maddie Friel is a social work student at Temple University, graduating in May 2025. Passionate about justice and advocacy, she aspires to work in the criminal legal system, using her voice to challenge systemic inequalities

Michael Cohen Artist, Writer, Filmmaker and singer-songwriter, Michael "Mickey" Cohen has been writing poetry since childhood.

Growing up in the turbulent 1960's and 70's in Brooklyn, NY Mickey expressed the emotional storm within him by writing poetry about the Vietnam War and the fight for dignity during the civil rights movement. The thrill of being published in his elementary school newspaper was the catalyst he needed for liftoff and the rest, as they say is history!

Cohen enjoyed a long career producing movies and content for television before shifting his focus to his love for art, he currently owns a gallery in the Village on High plaza, plays guitar, and sings in various local venues around town.

Mark Soifer passed away on June 6, 2021. A Vineland resident for 63 years, he commuted daily for over 45 years to Ocean City for his work as Director of Public Relations. He received many accolades and awards for his dedication in all facets of the community. In particular, he was honored to have a city park named after him. Known for his easy going personality and whimsical sense of humor, he originated & conducted many popular special events in Ocean City that attracted crowds to "America's Greatest Family Resort." He created characters such as Martin Z and Mollie Mollusk, Ocean City's mascots.

Although Mark worked tirelessly at his job, he also spent time on his passion of writing poetry & short stories, many having been published. He also mentored and encouraged many local Millville poets who continue to encourage and support younger generations of poets .

Robert Griffiths is a lifelong Cumberland County resident after graduating from Millville High School. He is a veteran, father, grandfather, and educator. Now retired, he taught Computer Sciences and CAD at St. Augustine's Prep where he was beloved by his students. He now spends his time supporting his children and their interests such as rebuilding antique cars and writing poetry.

Kevin Jordan was born in Diving Creek and raised in Mays Landing. He is a self-taught musician, artist, sculptor and wood carver who loves music, fishing, and time outdoors. He enjoyed his time being a roadie with The Billy Walton Band. He played percussion with The Indelible Groove and Overcast. He performed throughout South Jersey and Millville. You can find him at The Village on High creating art and assisting local artists, musicians, and vendors.

Mark Schardine is a New Jersey resident with a lifelong love of poetry, and the many pleasures it offers us. He believes that each of us is an heir to the remarkably beautiful tradition of poetry that previous generations have bequeathed to us, and seeks inspiration in works of the past. We must not merely imitate earlier works, but instead experiment with different forms of poetry to explore how old traditions and new experiences can lead to creativity.

In 2015, he published a French language book of his poems, entitled *Au bord des rêves*, and in 2019, it was followed by *Vers des horizons lointains* and in 2023 by *Illusions et espérance*. He has written three English language books, *Charm, Elegance, and Intrigue*, first published in 2019 and with a new edition in 2023, *As if in a Distant Dream*, published in 2020, and *Under Watchful Eyes* in 2022

Renee Rasinger, Cumberland County resident, is a poet, writer, jewelry maker, creativity coach and Edgar Allen Poe freak. She hosted River Rimes, a former poetry slam and open-mic in Bridgeton for a number of years. She has written for Serendipity, Down Jersey and other local publications. She authored the bi-monthly column "*Conjuring Creativity*" for Inferno. Her poetry has been published in *Platypus's Dreams* and *L'Espirit*. She is currently putting together a poetry book and is writing a historical fiction novel.

Alma Cole Pesiri first published poem was in a Salem High School newspaper. Where she also wrote on the yearbook staff, and co-wrote the class song. At a major glass manufacturing company, she penned co-worker bios and technical articles.

She creates collage-type poems, such as a balance scale, each side holding half the poem. She gained prizes from Cumberland County Older Americans Art Exhibit for photographs. Short story, "Look at Me" (based on a painful teen-age experience) gained an award from Montclair State College. Publication and readings include *Singles Scene, in AZ*, *What's In Atlantic City Magazine*, *NJ Poetry Society*, *Haddonfield Speaks*, *Paterson Literary Review*, *Chalfont/Steer Wilson Series*, *Frogpond*, and *Beach Bards Summer Series*.

www.ingramcontent.com/pod-product-compliance
Lightning Source LLC
Chambersburg PA
CBHW060220050426
42446CB00013B/3125